THE EASY PIANO COLLECTION

MOZART

GOLD

Published by:
Chester Music Limited
14-15 Berners Street, London V

Exclusive Distributor
Music Sales Corporatio
257 Park Avenue South, New York, NY 10010, U
Music Sales Limited,
Distribution Centre, Newmarket Road, Bury St Edmu
Music Sales Pty Limited,
120 Rothschild Avenue, Rosebery, NSW 2

Order No. CH72292
ISBN 978-1-84772-050-4
This book © Copyright 2007 by Chester Music.

Edited by Jessica Williams.
Arranging and engraving supplied by Camden Music.
Cover design by the Design Corporation.

Printed in the United States of America.

Your Guarantee of Quality:
As publishers, we strive to produce every book to the highest commercial standards.
The music has been freshly engraved and carefully designed to minimize
awkward page turns to make playing from it a real pleasure.
Particular care has been given to specifying acid-free, neutral-sized
paper made from pulps which have not been elemental chlorine bleached.
This pulp is from farmed sustainable forests and was produced
with special regard for the environment.
Throughout, the printing and binding have been planned to ensure a sturdy,
attractive publication which should give years of enjoyment.
If your copy fails to meet our high standards, please inform us and we will gladly replace it.

www.musicsales.com

CHESTER MUSIC
part of the Music Sales Group

London/New York/Paris/Sydney/Copenhagen/Berlin/Madrid/Tokyo

Air in E♭ major
Page 5

Allelujah (from 'Exsultate Jubilate' K165)
Page 6

Ave Verum Corpus (K618)
Page 10

Clarinet Concerto in A major (K622 Adagio)
Page 14

Contredanse in G major
Page 16

Der Vogelfänger bin ich ja ('Birdcatcher's Song') (from 'The Magic Flute' K620)
Page 17

Divertimento No.17 (K334 Minuet)
Page 18

Duettino in A♭ major
Page 20

Eine kleine Nachtmusik (K525 1st movement theme)
Page 22

German Dance 'The Sleigh Ride'
Page 21

Horn Concerto in E♭ major (K495 Rondo)
Page 26

Kyrie Eleison
Page 30

Là Ci Darem La Mano (from 'Don Giovanni' K527)
Page 13

Lacrimosa (from 'Requiem' K626)
Page 32

Laudate Dominum (from 'Vesperae solennes de Confessore' K339)
Page 34

Minuet (from 'Don Giovanni' K527)
Page 36

Minuet in F major (K2)
Page 37

A Musical Joke (K522)
Page 38

Piano Concerto No.21 in C major 'Elvira Madigan' (K467 Andante)
Page 40

Piano Sonata in A major (K331 Andante Grazioso theme)
Page 41

Piano Sonata in C major (Theme)
Page 42

Piano Sonata in G major (K283 1st movement)
Page 44

Polonaise (from 'Viennese Sonatina No.5')
Page 48

Romance (from 'Eine kleine Nachtmusik' K525)
Page 52

'Sonata Facile' in C major (K545 Allegro theme)
Page 49

Symphony No.40 in G minor (K550 1st movement: Allegro molto)
Page 54

Symphony No.41 'The Jupiter' (K551 3rd movement: Minuet)
Page 56

Variations on 'Ah! Vous Dirai-je, Maman' (K265)
Page 58

Voi Che Sapete (from 'The Marriage of Figaro' K492)
Page 62

Wolfgang Amadeus Mozart

Wolfgang Amadeus Mozart was born in the city of Salzburg on 27th January 1756 and, though he lived a short life, became one of the most influential and highly respected composers and performers of all time. His sister, Maria 'Nannerl' Anna was also a brilliant musician and his father Leopold was a talented court musician, composer and violin teacher.

Even as a toddler, Mozart was picking out tunes by ear and by the age of five was composing his own pieces. Leopold Mozart recognised these rare gifts and promptly took his children on a series of grand tours, displaying their prodigious talents to the rest of the world. After trips to places such as Vienna and Munich in 1762, Paris in 1763, London in 1764 and Holland in 1766, Mozart finally returned to Salzburg in 1766, having already written many compositions including the *Minuet in F Major (K2)*.

Mozart's output from 1769–77 increased at an incredible rate, and he produced nearly 300 compositions from sacred to symphonic, including the *Piano Sonata No.5 in G (K283)* and over 20 symphonies. During this time he also managed to tour Italy, where he was honoured with a knighthood in Rome, and revisited Vienna and Munich.

On 9th July 1772, Mozart was formally employed as Konzertmeister at the Salzburg Court, a position that had previously been unpaid. The following year saw the composition and performance of the celebrated *Exsultate Jubilate*, the final movement of which is included in this book.

Mozart was frustrated at his attempts to leave Salzburg, but eventually managed to embark on a trip with his mother late in 1777, visiting Mannheim and Paris. Here, amongst other things, he composed the variations on *'Ah! Vous Dirai-je Maman'*, the theme of which is better known as the nursery rhyme *'Twinkle, Twinkle, Little Star'*.

Mozart's mother Anna Maria became ill and died in Paris in 1778. Mozart then travelled on to Munich alone, returning to Salzburg in 1779 where he composed the *Divertimento No.17 (K334)*. Although terribly affected by his mother's death, he was able to put his grief to one side and began to devote all his energies to composing.

1780 saw the creation of the magnificent *Vesperae solennes de Confessore*. In 1782 he married Contanze Weber in St. Stephen's Cathedral, having decided to settle permanently in Vienna. The Mozarts finally visited Salzburg again in the summer of 1783. While he may have felt some trepidation about Constanze meeting his autocratic father, Wolfgang must have been overjoyed to see his sister for the first time in many years.

In 1783, the Mozarts had their first child, Raimund Leopold, but he died after only two months. They went on to have a further five children, three of whom died in infancy. Despite these sorrowful events, Mozart's first years in Vienna were musically and financially very successful. This was largely because of Mozart's subscription concert series' in which he played and conducted his own pieces such as the *Piano Concerto in C Major (K467)* also known as *'Elvira Madigan'* after the film in which the piece features.

Mozart was also well known among his musical colleagues, often holding soirées and playing chamber music with them. They included the great composer Haydn, who is reported to have said to Leopold Mozart, 'Before God, I tell you that your son is the greatest composer known to me in person or by reputation'.

In 1786 Mozart wrote the opera *The Marriage of Figaro (K492)* and was the toast of both Vienna and Prague. Following this success he prepared a further collaboration with his preferred librettist, Lorenzo Da Ponte, on the subject of Don Juan—*Don Giovanni (K527)* was premiered in Prague in October 1787 and was a success. However the response in Vienna was cooler, the monarch Joseph II saying that it was 'not the food for the teeth of my Viennese'. Around this time also, Mozart composed the serenade *Eine kleine Nachtmusik (K525)*. Mozart's father had died earlier that year in Salzburg, and it must have seemed as if the final link to his birthplace had been severed. Following this, Mozart composed *A Musical Joke (K522)* which mercilessly parodies the poor taste and playing of the Salzburg musicians which he had found so frustrating in his youth.

Having moved to cheaper lodgings in the suburbs in the summer of 1788, Mozart found fresh inspiration and composed his final three symphonies including *Symphony No.41 'The Jupiter' (K551)*. Despite Mozart's deepening financial crisis there seems to have been no reward or commission for this mammoth task—it appears that he composed them solely for his own gratification.

Although he was still experiencing modest success in Vienna, Mozart was far from financially stable. He owed a lot of money, mostly to his Masonic brethren who always lent money. In his final year, Mozart seemed to go into overdrive, working on three operas (including *The Magic Flute (K620)*), the *Clarinet Concerto in A (K622)* and the *Requiem (K626)*, which remained unfinished at his death in December 1791. Even in this hive of activity he still found time to complete a small motet, *Ave Verum Corpus (K618)*, as a gift to a choirmaster in Baden.

There can be few composers of whom it could be said that their influence stretched far and wide within their own lifetime *and* well into the centuries that followed their death. When that influence came from such a short life, it is all the more remarkable.

Michael Ahmad, April 2007

Air in E♭ major

Composed by Wolfgang Amadeus Mozart

Andantino

Allelujah
(from 'Exsultate Jubilate' K165)

Composed by Wolfgang Amadeus Mozart

Allegro non troppo

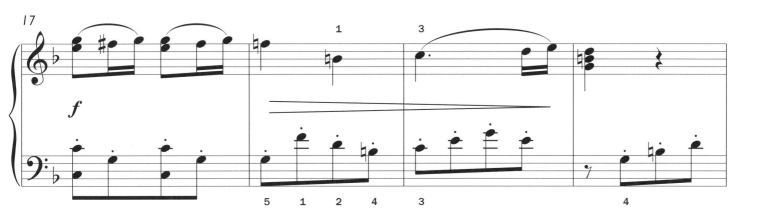

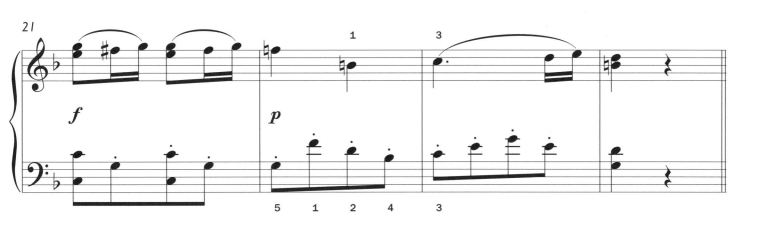

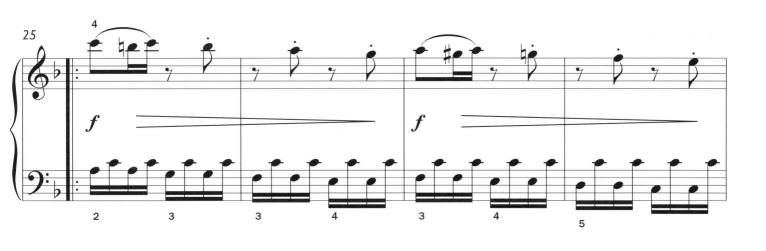

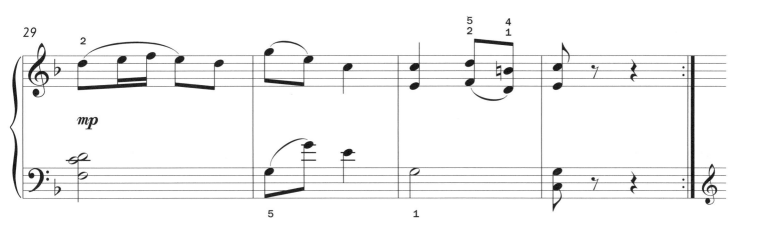

Ave Verum Corpus
(K618)

Composed by Wolfgang Amadeus Mozart

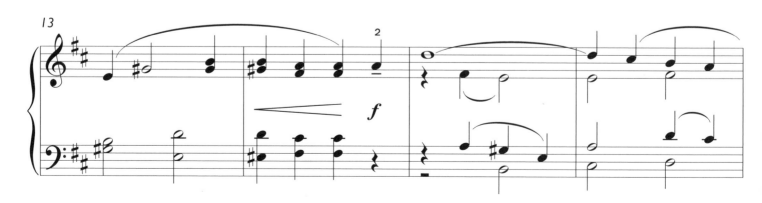

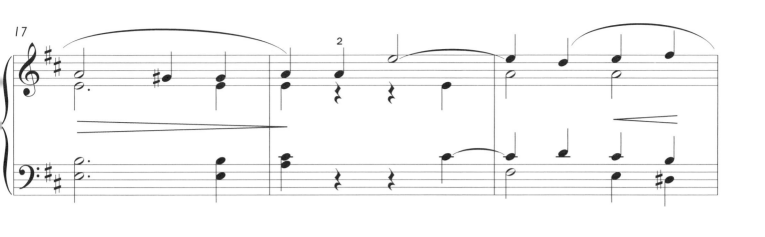

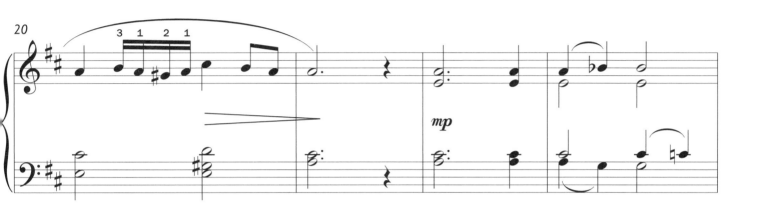

Là Ci Darem La Mano
(from 'Don Giovanni' K527)

Composed by Wolfgang Amadeus Mozart

Moderato

Clarinet Concerto in A major
(K622 Adagio)

Composed by Wolfgang Amadeus Mozart

Contredanse in G major

Composed by Wolfgang Amadeus Mozart

Der Vogelfänger bin ich ja ('Birdcatcher's Song')
(from 'The Magic Flute' K620)

Composed by Wolfgang Amadeus Mozart

* The small notes indicate the original version which can be played instead of the simplified version if preferred.

Divertimento No.17
(K334 Minuet)

Composed by Wolfgang Amadeus Mozart

Duettino in A♭ major

Composed by Wolfgang Amadeus Mozart

German Dance 'The Sleigh Ride'

Composed by Wolfgang Amadeus Mozart

Eine kleine Nachtmusik
(K525 1st movement theme)

Composed by Wolfgang Amadeus Mozart

25

Horn Concerto in E♭ major
(K495 Rondo)

Composed by Wolfgang Amadeus Mozart

D.S. al Coda

⊕ Coda

Kyrie Eleison

Composed by Wolfgang Amadeus Mozart

Lacrimosa
(from 'Requiem' K626)

Composed by Wolfgang Amadeus Mozart

Laudate Dominum
(from 'Vesperae solennes de Confessore' K339)

Composed by Wolfgang Amadeus Mozart

Minuet
(from 'Don Giovanni' K527)

Composed by Wolfgang Amadeus Mozart

Tempo di minuetto

Minuet in F major
(K2)

Composed by Wolfgang Amadeus Mozart

A Musical Joke
(K522)

Composed by Wolfgang Amadeus Mozart

Allegro vivace

Piano Concerto No.21 in C major
'Elvira Madigan'
(K467 Andante)

Composed by Wolfgang Amadeus Mozart

Andante

Piano Sonata in A major
(K331 Andante Grazioso theme)

Composed by Wolfgang Amadeus Mozart

Andante Grazioso

Piano Sonata in C major
(Theme)

Composed by Wolfgang Amadeus Mozart

Piano Sonata in G major
(K283 1st movement)

Composed by Wolfgang Amadeus Mozart

Allegro

Polonaise
(from 'Viennese Sonatina No.5')

Composed by Wolfgang Amadeus Mozart

Andantino

'Sonata Facile' in C major
(K545 Allegro theme)

Composed by Wolfgang Amadeus Mozart

Romance
(from 'Eine kleine Nachtmusik' K525)

Composed by Wolfgang Amadeus Mozart

Symphony No.40 in G minor
(K550 1st movement: Allegro molto)

Composed by Wolfgang Amadeus Mozart

Symphony No.41 'The Jupiter'
(K551 3rd movement: Minuet)

Composed by Wolfgang Amadeus Mozart

Allegretto

Variations on 'Ah! Vous Dirai-je, Maman'
(K265)

Composed by Wolfgang Amadeus Mozart

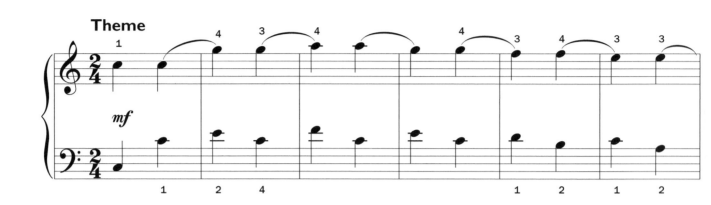

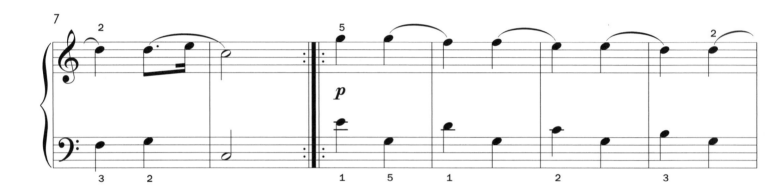

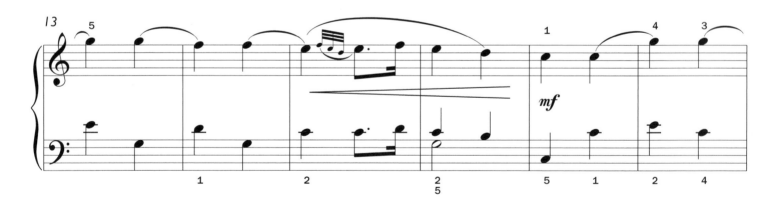

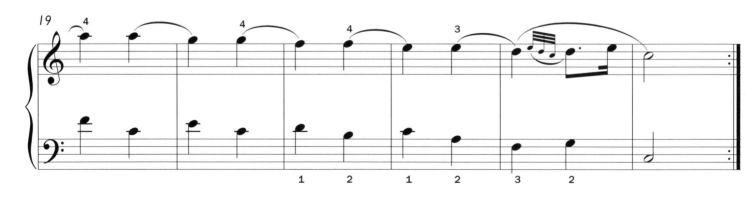

Voi Che Sapete
(from 'The Marriage Of Figaro' K492)

Composed by Wolfgang Amadeus Mozart

D.C. al Coda

Coda

123456789